INVERNESS REMEMBERED
VI

Published by
New Century Publishing Group

New Century
Publishing Group

INVERNESS REMEMBERED VI

Edited and Compiled by Willie Morrison

CONTRIBUTORS

William T Weatherspoon

Allan Cameron

Anne C MacKintosh

Beatrice Grigor

Christopher MacKenzie

Dorothy Ahearn

Edith Hill

Elanar Gruson

Eleanor Thomson

Ian Fraser

Jackie Sinclair

James Sutherland

Jamie Angus

Karen Hutchison

Linda Law

Margaret Gordon

Marjorie Stuart

Murdoch Smith

Rosemary McIlwraith

Vivien MacKintosh

Joan Clyne

Peter Home

Rory Macleod

M Nicoll

Karl Reid

J Wemyss

Murdo MacKenzie

Pat Munro

John Burnside

Elizabeth MacKenzie

Rosa Finlayson

Peter Chisholm

Robert McPhee

Jeff MacLeod

Pat Munro

Clem Watson

Anne McArthur

Helen Finlayson

Pat Munro

Lynn MacKenzie

Irene Macpherson

Harry Kelly

C MacDonald

Elsie Baxter

Isabel Munro

Betty Mackay

Graham MacDonald

Alan Simmons

P Cook

Rose Ann MacKenzie

Margaret Kelly

Iain Cameron

A Catalogue Record for this book is available from The British Library.

CONTENTS

INTRODUCTION

TIME seems to telescope in an alarming manner as one grows older and it scarcely seems a year since publication of the last volume of Inverness Remembered.

Once again the photographs from Inverness and district that we publish span several eras, from beyond living memory to occasions still well remembered.

The aim is not to celebrate the great events of byegone days in and around our former burgh, in this millennium promoted to city status, but to record a few random samples of how ordinary people lived, worked and took their pleasure in the less complicated days of yesteryear.

While it is inevitable that some photos of celebrities or members of the national and local great and good appear on our pages, by far the majority of people pictured are members of the modest majority, who went about their business day after day, year after year, with minimum fuss and often little recognition.

It's amazing how each year, so far, local folk and exiles have revisited their own or their ancestral past, and have emerged not only with many interesting photos, but also interesting stories to accompany them.

We give heartfelt thanks to all our contributors, including those who have contacted us to comment on or to correct captions for photos from earlier issues of Inverness Remembered.

Some contributors may not be mentioned here, as we tend to process photos on a first-come basis, but worry not, if your pictures do not appear in Inverness Remembered VI, we will do our best to ensure that they appear in Inverness Remembered VII. We still have at least 50 excellent photographs which will give an excellent start to that particular issue.

The right Macdonald

Last year's contributor James Macpherson, who sent in the photo on Page 22 of Inverness Remembered V, of a National Service squad of soldiers which had just completed training at the Cameron Barracks in early 1947, was also able to tell us that the politician of yesteryear in the forefront of the photo at the top of Page 68 was not former prime minister Ramsay Macdonald, as we had surmised, but a rather more mediocre parliamentarian of the same surname, who had distinguished himself greatly in earlier walks of life.

He was Sir Murdoch Macdonald the Inverness-born civil engineer who rose to such challenges as the construction of the mighty Aswan Dam in Egypt and who later entered Parliament as MP for Inverness-shire.

Born in 1866, Macdonald was educated at Dr Bell's Farraline Park School, now Inverness Public Library, where he later served as a "pupil teacher" for two years.

He joined the Highland Railway initially as a clerk, but was apprenticed to the company's chief engineer Murdoch Paterson. From 1890 he worked successively on construction of the Black Isle Railway, in charge of new line surveys and latterly as resident engineer on doubling of the main line between Blair Atholl and Dalnaspidal, but in 1898 left to work for the Egyptian Government. In 1902 he was appointed resident engineer on construction of the first Aswan Dam.

From 1907 Macdonald was appointed Egypt's director-general of reservoirs, a post he held for five years, until promoted under-secretary of state for public works and later adviser to the Ministry of

Public Works on irrigation and drainage works, posts he held until 1922. During the Great War, as a temporary colonel in the Royal Engineers, he advised on military constructions in Gallipoli during the abortive campaign against the Turks, and also on the defence of the Suez Canal, being mentioned in dispatches three times and created Companion of the Bath in 1917.

Knighted in 1914, Macdonald changed careers in 1922 when elected as Liberal Member of Parliament for Inverness-shire, a role in which he served adequately, but without great distinction, until 1950, when he was 83. His most noteworthy parliamentary accomplishment was to persuade the Scottish Secretary of the time to issue an order protecting the Loch Ness Monster, a phenomenon in which he was said to have believed firmly.

Sir Murdoch maintained his engineering interests, however, and in 1927 formed his Inverness-based firm of Sir Murdoch Macdonald & Partners, which among many contracts heightened the Aswan Dam and designed the 1961 Ness Bridge. In 1989 Macdonald & Partners became a core member of the multinational Mott Macdonald Group.

In 1899 he married Margaret Munro, by whom he had two sons. She died in 1956. Created a Fellow of the Royal Astronomical Society two years after his retirement from Parliament, Sir Murdoch died in 1957.

In the picture, Sir Murdoch is the man with the moustache and homburg hat fourth from the left.

Mr Macpherson, of Dochfour Drive, Inverness, whose first job after demob was with Macdonald & Partners, recalls: "He was a very clever man, but a mean old devil."

The scene of the photo, thought to date from the early 1930s, may have been the roof of the old burgh fire station, behind the Town House, and long demolished, Mr Macpherson thinks.

The man on the extreme left is identified by Mr Macpherson as lamplighter and auxiliary fireman Dot MacBeath, while third from the left is Duncan Macdonald, later firemaster. Third from the right is Firemaster Treasurer and on the far right, lamplighter and part-time fireman Alex Fraser. At that time the burgh's lamplighters made up the bulk of the local firefighting force, and local businessman Scott Don recalls that his father Andrew was appointed shortly before the war as joint lighting supervisor and firemaster.

Confusion on parade

It's of interest to note that another member of the National Service squad in which James Macpherson trained has also contacted Inverness Remembered.

Invernessian Alan MacLeod, now living in Edinburgh, confirms that the photo of the recruits was taken in February or March 1947, of the newly-trained group known as Waterloo Squad, when Cameron Barracks also accommodated what was known as 79 Primary Training Centre. Whether the number was allocated by the War Office deliberately or not, it was very appropriate, as the Cameron Highlanders were descended from the old 79th Regiment of byegone days.

Mr MacLeod tells us that the corporal and lance-corporal were named Roberts and Bowker respectively, and further recalls that out of 32 men in the squad, there were about eight MacLeods, with a similar number of MacDonalds. "Very confusing, and it required the addition of the last three digits of each man's number to identify individuals," he muses, adding: "To the best of my knowledge, I have not seen any of them since we were posted away from the Barracks, 63 years ago."

A plea to readers

As a footnote, may I also plead with every reader please, please, never throw to away old photographs of however apparently humble origin, without first examining them closely as evidence of social history.

Each is a unique snapshot of a moment in time which can never be recaptured if destroyed. Often, the more commonplace these photos, the better, as they give an insight into the lives of the great, almost forgotten majority.

Far too many old pictures have over the years been disposed of as being of no value, when in fact they might well have thrown interesting light on everyday life in the communities from which they originated.

So please look again at them in a different light, and if you have the know-how, why not scan them into a computer to save and improve for posterity.

Around Inverness of yesteryear

One of countless studies of the handsome old Suspension Bridge, photographed around 1920 from beside Inverness Castle, looking towards Ben Wyvis in the distance.

Inverness Town House pictured in the early inter-war period, with the YMCA building and Grant's Clan Tartan Warehouse in the foreground, and the Exchange beyond. Note the contrast between the horse-drawn cab and the motor car just visible in the right-hand lower corner.

INVERNESS CASTLE FROM RIVER. 212900.

A study of Inverness Castle, one of many from byegone days, taken from the riverside near Inverness Cathedral. It dates from around 1930, judging from the car just visible on the left.

This picture of the old Suspension Bridge from the 1950s shows something of the character Inverness riverside has lost, including on the right, Queen Mary's House and a corner of the former Caledonian Hotel, all brutally demolished nearly half-a-century ago to make way for what the pundits of the time called progress. It also demonstrates how much the UK has lost by way of industrial capacity, as almost all the cars visible in the photo are British-made, a phenomenon inconceivable in a study taken today.

The old Suspension Bridge, the original Caledonian Hotel and some of the picturesque riverside buildings sacrificed at the altar of development for the fast buck in the mid-20th Century are still visible in this view of the town centre from Friars' Shott, circa 1955

A busy day in Academy Street in 1961, snapped by Rory Macleod from its junction with Station Square, looking south towards Inglis Street. The cyclist seems to be in a hurry – perhaps a railwayman hastening to his work. Note Stewart's Restaurant, in a former church, with its distinctive rose window, which was supposed to have been incorporated in the new Eastgate Centre, but was somehow "overlooked" by the developers. Among the cars in the picture, all British-made, are a Vauxhall, a Ford Consul Mark II, an Austin Cambridge, a Jaguar and what looks like a pre-war Austin.

This photo was taken by Rory Macleod in 1960 at the point where tiny Young Street joins Tomnahurich Street. The Tarry Ile building remains, but Rossleigh's Garage, then the main Rootes Group dealership for the Highlands, has long been demolished to make way for a Tesco store, while Rootes Group vehicles are also a memory. A new Hillman Minx Mark III, Rootes' most popular make in those days, stands outside the garage, while on the right, the tail of a parked Vauxhall Wyvern or Velox is visible. Note the presence of no less than six cyclists, including three women, travelling three abreast.

This aerial photograph, submitted by Robert McPhee, can be dated fairly precisely to around 1964, as the south end of Bridge Street had just been flattened to make way for the dreary grey present-day concrete excrescences which replaced such picturesque buildings as the Workmen's Club, the Police Station and Castle Tolmie.

A view from the corner of Grant Street, looking towards South Kessock and the Black Isle on a fine day in the 1950s. The small Ford Thames 10 cwt van and the electric milk float indicate the period. Note the relative lightness of traffic, compared to today, with cyclists riding three abreast and a young woman walking fearlessly along the roadway.

A fine study of Culloden House, Inverness, in its heyday as a private residence. It lies little more than four miles from the city centre. Note the width of the little lake, then large enough to float the small boat at the right of the picture, today reduced to a modest duck pond. The former seat of Clan Forbes is now a luxury hotel.

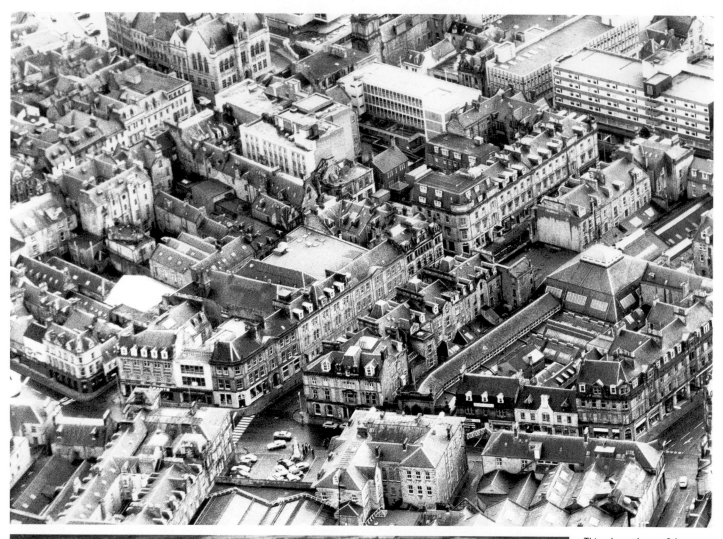

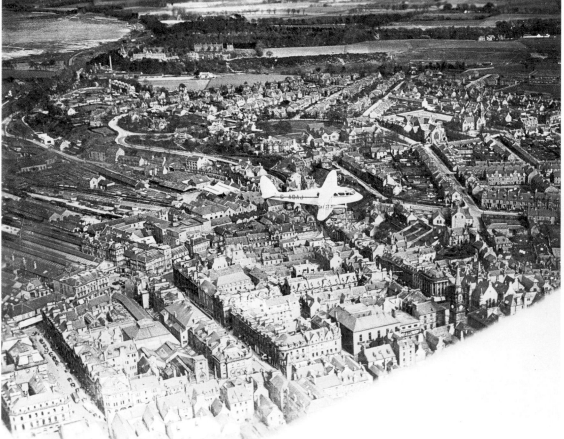

This clear photo of Inverness town centre was taken on a summer Sunday in 1972 at 500 feet, from a Cessna 150 aircraft, by aero enthusiast Clem Watson of Nairn. The pilot was Frank Ogg, owner of the then Strathspey Flying Club, based at Dalcross. Says Clem: "Note the Salvation Army band round the Cameron Highlander memorial." In the picture also are the former Royal Hotel in Academy Street, Arnott's department store in Union Street, the roof of the Victorian Market and in the top left-hand corner, the Town House.

Another view of Inverness town centre, taken nearly four decades earlier in 1933, by photographer Sandy McLaren, who has signed his name on the back of the original, along with the year and the type of aircraft, a Dragon Rapide, registered G-ADAJ, said to be pioneering aviator Captain Eric Fresson's favourite, and almost certainly flown by him when this study was taken.

Early days recalled

This clutch of photographs, along with several in the section headed Relaxation and Entertainment, was lent to Inverness Remembered by Edith Hill, of Innes Street, Inverness, formerly Edith Fraser. They belong to her mother Peggy Fraser, now 91, who has lived at 29 Cauldeen Road, Hilton, since the day she and her young family moved there in July 1951.

"She's still as bright as a button and can tell some great tales of the town and the people with whom she worked, mostly in hotels, so she knew everyone," says Mrs Hill.

Edith's grandparents lived at 9 Queen Street, and she lived with them as a child. "Then we moved to temporary accommodation in 'Hut 25' – a converted Nissen hut – at Bught Park for short time, before moving to Hilton, she recalls.

Robert Mackay, of 9 Queen Street, Inverness, Edith Hill's grandfather, in his uniform as chauffeur to Miss MacKenzie of Stratton Farm in the 1920s, in the days when employing one's own uniformed driver was a particular status symbol. Miss MacKenzie considered him as much a friend as an employee.

Edith Fraser, now Edith Hill, pictured with her twin brothers, Barry (left) and David, in 1951, shortly before the family moved to Hilton.

David and Barry Fraser with Great-granny Ross outside "Hut 25" in 1950. The background shows the Bught Stadium.

Family friend Betty Darling, wife of soldier Peter Darling, with her first son Peter outside 9 Queen Street in 1961. Note the comfortable pram of that time, probably a popular Silver Cross, so different in design from today's baby buggies. Peter Jnr also became a soldier, like his dad, and for a time the two served together.

Barry's and David Fraser's second birthday celebrations, held at "Hut 25" at Bught, Park, respectively being held by Betty Mackay and Betty Moore.

Inverness at work

The driver (left) of this engine, taken around 40 years ago, is lifetime railwayman and football enthusiast George "Butch" Sinclair, but we have no information about the other man, possibly a visiting VIP.

The last survivor of the famous series of Highland Railway Jones goods engines, HR 103, built in 1894, pictured at the long-demolished Inverness "Round House" engine shed around 60 years ago. The engine survives to this day in the Glasgow Museum of Transport. The railwaymen photographed with the classic locomotive are, rear, from left: George "Butch" Sinclair, Willie Mackenzie "Red Will"; front, from left: Alex Dowling, Fred MacSween, Jimmy Paterson, foreman.

This study of Inverness Burgh Police Force's modest traffic department recalls an age when patrol cars were invariably of British make – in this case an Austin A110 Mk II Westminster, a model phased out a year after this photo was taken in 1967. Pictured, from left, are: Sergeant Eric Lockwood, Constables Archie Campbell, Davy Grey, George Grant, typist Madeline Sutherland, Sergeant John Ross and Constables Jim Sutherland, Willie Maclean and Ken Macleod. The following year the burgh force amalgamated with Inverness County Constabulary.

Constables Davy Grey (left) and Jimmy Sutherland of the new Northern Constabulary were snapped on motor cycle patrol on the old A9 road near the former Daviot Police Station in 1976.

Preparing comprehensively for winter patrols around 1978, with their new Range Rovers, are from left, Northern Constabulary members Constable Murdo Sutherland, Chief Inspector Dan Green and Constable Jimmy Sutherland.

Electricians from Inverness-based Queensgate Electrical braved heavy snows to carry out essential maintenance tasks at Tomatin Distillery as this photo from the mid-1950s shows. Standing by his Austin van, in the middle of a snowdrift his own height is one of the firm's employees, Tommy Ross. The vehicle's registration, BST 607 indicates that it was registered shortly after the war.

Another snowy photograph showing the old access road to Tomatin Distillery, with Queensgate Electrical's electricians Donnie Wemyss (left) and Murdoch Smith posing beside a huge snowdrift to demonstrate how difficult their journey had been.

These workers were snapped taking a welcome break from helping to build the swing bridge over the Caledonian Canal at Millerton, Tomnahurich, in 1938, to ease the flow of traffic on the then recently reconstructed Inverness – Fort William Road. Sitting at the front is Dan Macdonald (1908-87), whose granddaughter submitted the picture, while fourth from the left at the back is George Welsh, who later became Dan's next-door neighbour for many years in Smith Avenue. Note the "bunnets" the men of that period all wore. The photo is by P Craigie Fleming, Press and General Photographer, 36 Friars' Street, Inverness, of whom little is now remembered, except that he operated in Inverness in the inter-war period and was working in Stornoway around 1917 and 1918. This picture is one of a set taken by Fleming for the bridge contractor, Sir William Arrol & Co, to show progress during the various stages of construction.

A photo to delight historic railway buffs, of a maintenance squad in a workshop at Inverness railway station between the wars. Third from the left is Peter "Pat" Shivas, born 1902, then living at Carlton Terrace, and latterly in Hawthorn Drive, whose daughter Pat Munro submitted this photograph. Can any of our readers identify others pictured here?

James Fraser was born at Kilmorack, near Beauly, in 1883, a member of a large family whose father died when he was only 10. He had to leave school early and became a coachman, then one of the 20th Century's early chauffeur-mechanics, before serving in army motor transport in the Great War. On demob he resumed work as a chauffeur to a prominent Inverness businessman, but had to leave for a post as lorry driver with builder James Campbell, which did not take him away from home overnight, after his wife Jessie took ill. He is pictured here around 1932, during construction of an extension at the Royal Northern Infirmary, with a lorry belonging to James Campbell. James died in 1954, with a proud record of having only been unemployed for half a day during his working life. The lorry, ST 5871, is described in the old Inverness-shire County Council's rather sketchy vehicle records as being a "goods", first registered on 31 July 1929, and although the make is not given, as it ought to have been, the diamond shape on the bonnet indicates that it is a US-designed Chevrolet, of a kind manufactured shortly afterwards in Luton under the famous name of Bedford.

Staff of York Drive Laundry, Bellfield Park, snapped in the 1960s.

There's little information about this photograph, thought to be of a rather sombre occasion, apart from the facts that it was taken by the late indomitable Sandy McLaren of Star Photos, which dates it to at least 60 years old, and that the motor-boat, according to a note on the back, is called Priscilla. The police officer is believed to be dredging the River Ness for a body.

This photo of urgent riverbank repairs, taken in the early 1950s, demonstrates the capricious nature of the River Ness throughout the ages. A huge chunk of the bank, in front of Dixie Villa, the former customs house in Anderson Street, had been washed away by a combination of strong spring tides and overflowing from Loch Ness. The lorry parked precariously near the edge, owned by A Ross & Sons, Contractors, Inverness, is an Austin K Series tipper truck, a type which first appeared shortly before World War II, went into mass production for the civilian market after hostilities and like its very similar rival, the Bedford O Series, remained popular with contractors for long afterwards.

Members of staff of the old Caledonian Hotel, in their uniforms, pictured for posterity in the 1960s.

Hospitals and nurses

Inverness has long been well served by hospitals and medical staff, as befits the Highland Capital. This photo of the Royal Northern Infirmary in the 1930s, when it was still the Highlands' principal hospital, is thankfully little different from a picture taken in today's digital age. The car in the foreground, with a badge reminiscent of a Riley of that period, but merely described as a "coupe" of 15.7 horsepower in the Inverness-shire registration records, bears the number plate ST 6687 and was first registered to Dr William Bethune, 3 Union Street, Inverness, on 27 July 1931. The only well-known cars of that period with engines of exactly that horsepower were the Humber 16/50 and Hillman Wizard, both from the then expanding Rootes empire, so it could possibly be one of these. Can any classic motor buff elucidate or can any reader remember?

This is what a smart theatre staff nurse at the Royal Northern Infirmary looked like in 1944. Margaret McWilliam may have been young and pretty, but doesn't her immaculate appearance inspire confidence belying her years?

A bit more casual were these student nurses at the entrance to the Nurses' Home, Raigmore Hospital, in 1972, from left: Cathie Ann Smith, Donna MacLeod, Beatrice MacBean.

Ward 7 staff at the Royal Northern Infirmary at Christmas 1974, from left Mrs Fraser, Christine Oman and Beatrice MacBean.

Sunny smiles on a wintry day in 1948 from this sextet of student nurses, pictured outside the Royal Northern Infirmary. They are, from left: Marie Chisholm, Mary Lumsden, Isabel MacLennan, Christine Sutherland, N Green, N McGruer.

A study of the former Culduthel Hospital for infectious diseases by Isabel MacLennan, now Isabel Munro, living in Inverness. Mrs Munro spent 29 years at Culduthel Hospital, ending her career as senior night sister. She escorted the last patient from the hospital, which closed in 1989, to the new infectious diseases ward at Raigmore Hospital, just before she retired from nursing. "I was very sad when it closed," recalls Mrs Munro, who was born near Cannich and brought up at Lochluichart, Ross-shire,. "It was a lovely place to work in, with such a happy atmosphere, where all the staff got on so well together." All of the hospital but Culduthel House, which formed its core, and part of which is just visible, was subsequently knocked down to make way for a housing development, the old house itself being converted into luxury flats.

Students of the nursing preliminary training school at Raigmore Hospital in 1967, rear, from left: Michael MacDonald, unidentified, unidentified, Dorothy Ewan, Janice MacDonald; front, from left: three unidentified, Dorothy Redmond, now Ahearn, who submitted his photo, and Amy - .

A grocer's progress

Master grocer Jimmy Christison, accompanied by his wife Cathy and three young children, moved to Inverness from Edinburgh in 1934 to become manager of the Maypole Dairy in High Street, located close to where Henderson the jeweller is now. In addition to selling dairy products, it was also a popular general grocery store, in those pre-supermarket days.

Called up into the forces in 1941, aged 35, Jimmy could have sought exemption for medical reasons, but decided to do his bit and joined the army. Despite living on her own with a young family during Jimmy's absence, big-hearted Cathy still managed to care also for a tiny evacuee girl from a deprived part of London.

Captured at Tobruk, North Africa, in 1942, Jimmy was a prisoner of war in Italy and Germany for the next three years, and resumed his civilian post on demob. He continued as manager of the Maypole until around 1960, when he opened a general store in St Margaret's Road, Dalneigh, taking with him two of his former staff, Bunty Mackenzie and Margaret Miller. Ill-health forced him to retire from the business in 1974. He died in 1991.

His youngest daughter, Karen Hutchison, tells us that at Christmas 1934, in a recess at the front door of the Maypole, her father put a table with a tartan cloth, with a whisky bottle filled with cold tea, and some black bun and fruit cake. The cake certainly sold, and Karen still has a letter from Maypole's head office, revealing that his branch was national top for sales, with orders of 5,645 lb – around 2.5 tons - over the three-week seasonal period.

The sequel came in January, when he was reprimanded by head office, which had received a complaint from the Temperance Society of Inverness, complaining about the fake whisky bottle and "the demon drink".

Karen also recalls how in those faraway days, butter was patted into shape, cheese cut by a wire and commodities wrapped in brown paper, tied up with string.

This photo shows Jimmy Christison (right) in the 1950s, with members of his staff in the long-vanished High Street branch of Maypole Dairy, along with shelves packed with commodities on offer. Bunty Mackenzie, who subsequently moved to St Margaret's Road with him, is standing next to him, while Margaret Miller is in the middle. His daughter Karen says the lady third from the right was called Dorcas Duncan, who used to babysit for her, and whom Karen thinks may still live in Dalneigh. She also thinks the lady third from the left was called Cathy, and that she left to work in Asher's bakery.

Jimmy Christison pictured in the High Street branch of Maypole Dairy along with some his comprehensive range of stock. Note the Maypole Savings Club poster on the wall behind him.

In this picture Jimmy is pictured presenting long-term employee Margaret Miller with a cheque and a watch for her loyal work, just before he retired from his business in St Margaret's Road.

From delivery boy to sailor

The bread delivery man driving a horse-drawn Burnett's van in this picture from the early 1930s was Cecil Fraser, his first job after leaving Farraline Park School in 1929.

Four years later Cecil joined the Royal Navy, in which he subsequently served throughout World War II. In civilian life he became a storeman at Inverness Motor Company, and also worked as a barman at the Glenmhor and Drumossie Hotels. These photos of Cecil with the van and in naval uniform were submitted by his son-in-law Allan Cameron.

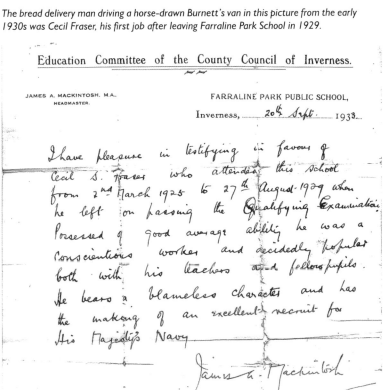

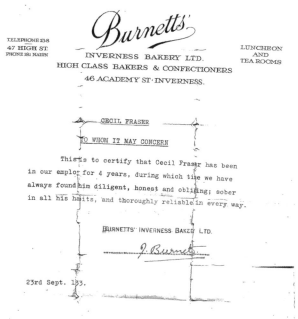

Cecil Fraser's references from Farraline Park School and Burnett's Bakery for the Royal Navy.

A veteran cyclist's memories

Lillias Kerr, the lady pictured with her terrier Paddy on the last of the Caledonian Canal paddle steamers, PS Gondolier, was still very much alive in her native Edinburgh, as Inverness Remembered VI was in course of preparation. Lillias and her late husband Richard spent many cycling holidays in the Highlands of the 1930s, often covering some of the roughest drove roads on their sturdy tandem. She had, however abandoned her cycle temporarily when this photo was taken in June 1939, as she was expecting her first child Robin, and was travelling in a less energetic manner from Fort Augustus to Inverness. Sadly the Gondolier, by then 73 years old, left the canal forever three months later, shortly after the outbreak of World War II. After the sinking of the battleship HMS Royal Oak in Scapa Flow by the German submarine U-47, Gondolier was requisitioned by the Admiralty, towed to Orkney and sunk as a blockship at one of the entrances to the Flow, to prevent further incursions by U-boats, pending construction of the Churchill Barriers. This photo was submitted by Lillias's daughter Elanar Gruson, who lives at Balnain, Glenurquhart.

Lillias Kerr is the farthest-away member of this trio pictured pushing cycles up a rough Highland track on a summer day in 1934. Her husband Richard is immediately in front. We do not have the name of the third member of the party, whose wife is thought to have taken the picture. They were making for the youth hostel at Balnain, Glenurquhart, coincidentally close to where her daughter Elanar Gruson now lives.

Another photograph from 1934, of the redoubtable Lillias Kerr with her trusty tandem cycle, taken at the Well of the Seven Heads, Loch Oich.

Coronation Year fever

Coronation fever was abroad in Inverness in 1953, when Queen Elizabeth was crowned, and many streets held their own parties to celebrate. It seems from this rare street party programme for Lochalsh Road (Upper), that this particular street might even have held two parties. It is particularly interesting to note how much real community spirit was present at the time, with both old and young being well catered for.

Britain was hauling itself out of the slough of postwar austerity, rationing had largely ended, and the population of Britain was starting to enjoy a modest measure of prosperity by the time these children of Primary 7 at Merkinch School were photographed at he dawn of the modern Elizabethan era in Coronation Year, 1953. The young folk here are, rear, from left: W Mackay, Syd Grant, D Cymbalist, Ian Ennis, Ali Mackay, Lyall MacRobb, Al Corbett, Vic Fridge, Norman Rothie, Charlie Fielden, Christopher Mackenzie; middle row, from left: Tom Walker, Brenda Quinn, unidentified. Fiona MacBean, Kay Munro, unidentified, Elizabeth MacKenzie, unidentified, Pat Whitecross, Nancy Macpherson, Jim Beaton; front, from left: D Smith, unidentified, Thomasina MacSween, Irene Shand, unidentified, Doris Mearns, Winnie Rose, unidentified, unidentified, Phyllis Wiseman, Kathleen Forbes, Ken Bussey.

A large part of Dalneigh housing estate still awaited completion when these two Coronation celebration photos were taken in June 1953, while the slopes of Craig Phadrig were innocent of the huge mass of dwellings which encroached on them in the second half of the 20th Century. World War II was only eight years past, and the age of austerity was still some time short of the "never had it so good" era, but everybody here seemed to be enjoying the event. The first picture is mainly of local children, while adults predominate in the second.

Coronation year school memories

One of the many classes in Merkinch School in Coronation Year, 1953, sent in by pupil of yesteryear Harry Kelly. Among those pictured, not in order, are, rear row: Douglas Mearns, Robbie Burns, Dave Mackie, Laurence Young, Leslie – , Miss McQueen; middle row: Finlay -, - Snowie, Ina Gunn, Charlie Watt, Harry Kelly, Fred Warburton; front: Myrtle Williams, Beryl MacDonald.

Another Coronation Year photo of Merkinch School pupils, submitted by reader Elsie Baxter.

The modern school so quickly replaced

The rapid post-war growth of Inverness, coupled with an increasing demand for secondary school accommodation, led to the erection of Millburn Junior Secondary School.

Located close to the old Mill Burn, from which it took its name, it welcomed its first intake of pupils in August 1961, under its first headmaster, John M Mathieson.

The school was subsequently opened officially on St Andrew's Day of that year by Murdo Morrison, former Director of Education for Inverness-shire. Mr Morrison, at that time 89 years old, maintained an interest in the school's development until his death at the age of 102.

The school's role changed rapidly in its first decade from a junior secondary to a comprehensive. A massive extension of its catchment area, including much of that of the former Inverness Royal Academy, saw the roll of 206 in 1961 rise to a maximum of 1,670 in 1976 and settle to around 950 by 1985. In August 2010 the roll numbered around 1,080, with 115 teaching staff.

The original school, built with minimal regard to quality or aesthetic appearance, in the manner of many a postwar construction, was bedevilled throughout its life both by maintenance problems and shortage of space. This led to the erection of an even uglier box-like concrete and glass extension, in typical Scottish Education Department-approved 1960s style, and later to a cluster of "temporary" huts springing up around its campus.

Construction of a new, rather more visually appealing, and hopefully more durable Millburn Academy, began on the school playing fields in January 2007, and the old buildings were demolished soon after its completion the following year.

Millburn Academy, which in 2011 celebrates its half-century, has to date had four rectors – John M Mathieson, from 1961-72, William T Weatherspoon, (1972-89), Graham C Spence (1990-2007) and Delia Thornton since 2007. The school's motto, since its inception, has been Strive to Achieve, and despite the logistical problems of its early decades, it has lived fairly well up to this goal.

The site now occupied by Millburn Academy, many decades before the school's construction. Note in the foreground the old farm buildings, with just beyond, the once-famous Millburn Distillery, and to the right, perched on its prominent knoll, the Cameron Barracks, completed in 1886.

The original Millburn Junior Secondary School.

The first Millburn Junior Secondary School prefects of session 1961-62, with the first headmaster John M Mathieson.

Millburn Academy senior rugby team 1961- 62, pictured with physical education teacher John Barr.

Millburn Academy athletics team 1963-64, with teachers Colin Baillie and Pat Cumming.

Millburn Secondary School's hockey first XI of 1964, rear, from left: Cheryl Gordon, Phyllis Hall, unidentified, Pat Laing, Rosalind Mahoney, Mary Martin, Gladys Smith; front, from left: Dorothy Brown, Christine Redmond, unidentified, Dorothy Redmond, Freda Macrae.

This rugby team from 1966-67 played for Millburn Academy, but we have no information about the players, or what honours if any they lifted that season. Can any reader fill in the information?

Millburn Academy bridge team, which won the Scottish Schools Bridge Championship Cup in 1979, 1980 and 1981, with their tutor Ruaridh MacDonald, principal teacher of mathematics

Over the years Millburn Academy staged a number of musicals produced by deputy rector Robert Sharpe and principal music teacher Tom Anderson. This was the cast of Oliver, produced in 1983.

Millburn Academy girls' basketball team 1984-85, pictured with physical education teacher Pat Farquharson.

Viscount Tonypandy, Speaker of the House of Commons from 1976-83, visited the school in June 1986. He is seen here, centre, with rector William Weatherspoon and senior modern studies pupils.

These were the school prefects 25 years after the school's inception, with rector William Weatherspoon and depute rector Donald Black. The increase in the number of prefects reflects the increase in the school roll over the years.

The original Millburn Academy building, on the left of this picture taken in 1989, when it was already facing maintenance problems and lack of accommodation, is dwarfed by extensions to meet the changing nature of the school. All these buildings were demolished in 2009 after the new school was opened.

The rapid expansion of Millburn Academy school roll in the 1970s and 1980s led to the erection of temporary huts to provide essential accommodation. At one time during this period there were over 30 huts on the school campus.

A school trip to Switzerland

In July 1949, a small group of Inverness Royal Academy pupils and staff set off for a two-week trip to Switzerland.

They spent the first week at the Hotel Seeblick, in the tourist village of Aeschi, one of the many resorts in the Bernese Oberland, recalls Alan Simmons, then a senior Academy pupil, while for the second week they moved on to Zweisimmen, staying at the Hotel Bristol Terminus.

The event, says Alan, cost £20 a head – a substantial sum for those days – while he had £5 spending money.

It was clearly a most interesting fortnight for the youngsters, hiking in the foothills of the Oberland and sightseeing.

"An excellent experience," is Alan's verdict.

A group expedition of that kind over 60 years ago, especially from a Highland school, was quite an ambitious undertaking.

Britain and most of Europe were still recovering from the disastrous effects of World War II, which had only ceased four years before.

Of course neutral Switzerland, like Sweden, was relatively prosperous, each having profited from selling arms and equipment to both sides during the conflict, so the difference in living standards between the host country and austere Britain must have been quite a surprise for the young visitors.

The lads – from left: Alan Dempster, Alan Simmons, Kenny MacDiarmid, Lewis Nairn, Lal Robertson (teacher) John Sanderson.

A SCHOOL TRIP TO SWITZERLAND

A group photo of the Inverness Royal Academy pupils and staff who took part in the 1949 expedition.

Members of staff who accompanied the pupils – from left: Alec MacKenzie, Lal Robertson and Frank Cunningham.

Five members of the group - rear, from left: Alan Simmons, John Sanderson, Kenny MacDiarmid; front, Aithne Rogers, left, and Lewis Nairn.

A halt for a rest on the hike to Blue Lake.

Members of the group snapped as they were about to leave Basle, or Basel as it seems to be called today.

Some of the young travellers enjoyed a further thrill a few months later at the National Mod, held at Inverness in October 1949, as members of Inverness Royal Academy's winning country dance team. In the rear row, from left, are: Alan Simmons, who submitted this photo, Ewen (MacGregor?), John Sanderson; front from left: Jean (Douglas?), Aithne Rogers, Moira (MacDonald?), Margaret Oliver, Lewis Nairn. The brackets with question marks denote surnames of which Mr Simmons has some doubt.

Schooldays remembered

Half a century ago there were still several tiny primary schools on the outskirts of Inverness, like Culduthel School, now a private house a few hundred yards up the brae leading to Farr, from the present Inverness Royal Academy. In 1959 when this photo was taken, the Academy was still in the Crown district, and Culduthel School, under headmaster James Steele from Skye, was a flourishing little feeder primary. Dorothy Ahearn, then Redmond, who submitted this photo, had been able to tell us some of the names of those in it. Rear, from left: Christine Cormack, unidentified, Jean Matheson, unidentified, unidentified, Robert Russell, unidentified, unidentified, but possibly with the surname Kennedy, Linda Mackenzie; front, from left: Brian Rizza, Andrew Douglas (twin), unidentified, Dorothy Redmond (twin), June Tait, Christine Redmond (twin), Ann Stewart, Richard Douglas (twin).

Dorothy Redmond, aged five, at her desk in Culduthel School in 1955.

A safety first cum nature study trip to the Leachkin by Primary 7 pupils of Central Primary School, around 1955, with community police officers Jimmy Still (left) and John Ross. Would policemen be allowed to hold children's hands in this age of political correctness?

Inverness Royal Academy Class IIIC 1956. Among those in the photo are, rear, from left: D McLucas, Alan Scott, James Dean, Jack Grigor, Alastair Mackay; second row from left: Kenneth Bussey, Ian Mackintosh, Iain Jack, Alan Spence, Christopher Mackenzie, Derek McGinn, unidentified, Donald R Chisholm, Ray Morton, James George; third row, all unidentified; front row, from left: Catherine Gordon, Josephine Moran, unidentified, unidentified, unidentified, unidentified, unidentified, Joan Macdonald, Elizabeth Tuach, Hazel Macpherson.

The Second World War had ended barely two years before, and most staple commodities were still strictly rationed, when these Primary 1 youngsters, pictured here in the austerity period of 1947, took their first educational steps at Central School.

The youngsters in this photo of pupils at Central Primary School seem so young and fresh you might think they could never age, but if there are any survivors they will shortly qualify for their centenary greetings from the Queen, as it was taken around 1921. It was submitted by Eleanor Thomson of Firthview Avenue, whose grandmother, then Helen Macrae from King Street, is pictured sixth from the left in the second back row, with her hands on another girl's shoulder. Helen, who on marriage became a Macdonald and lived in Smith Avenue, was born in 1911 and was thought to be 10 at the time. Unusually for that time, the photographer was from the Dundee-based firm D & W Prophet, rather than one of the many good local snappers.

Pupils of Culcabock Primary School pictured around 1946 with their headmaster Mr Macleod.

Class 1A4 at Inverness High School 1963. In it are, rear, from left: Alex MacLeod, John MacRae, Derek Daley, William MacQueen, Malcolm MacDonald, Robert Wallace; second row from rear: Miss I Allen, form teacher, John Sutherland, Shenda MacDonald, Carol MacKenzie, Elizabeth MacGillivray, Helen Thomson, James Stewart; third row from rear: George Kirkpatrick, Andrew Mathieson, Margaret Williamson, Ellen Watt, Sheila Call, Michael Beeham, Tommy Anderson; front row: David MacMillan, Sandy Wilson, Helen MacIntosh, Linda Mellis, Heather Campbell, Linda Smith, Jane Pendreigh, Christine Paterson, Peter MacMillan.

This photo, submitted by Vivien Mackintosh, formerly MacRae, is of her Inverness High School class, with teacher Mrs Pollitt, taken in 1960 when she and her colleagues were near the end of their second year. Rear row, from left: Donald MacKenzie, Sandy MacArthur, Tom Cator, Alan Rae, Brian Campbell, Gerald Breau, Denis Grant, William Grant; third row, from left: Walter Smith, Donald Fraser, Roy Fraser, Brian Corbett, Donald Campbell, Ronnie Mitchell, Bernard Robertson, Alan Brown; second row, Jane Rose, Vivien MacRae, Valerie Kerr, Cherry MacKinnon, Ishbel Duncan, Flora MacRae, Margaret Kelly, Margaret Davidson, Irene Fraser, Elizabeth Watt; front row, sitting, from left: Rosemary White, Maria McNally, Moira MacGregor, Jean Galbraith, Pauline Bell, Christine Tasker, Lilian MacLeod, Valerie Gordon, Mary Crosbie, Margaret Jeans; front, sitting, cross-legged, from left: Kenneth Macpherson, James MacAdam, Donald Calder.

Inverness High School prefects of 1959-60, pictured with headmaster William G Johnston and lady superintendent Isobel Swanston. Rear row, from left: Calum Macdonald, Robert English, Campbell Welsh, William Paterson, Ronnie Mackenzie, Duncan MacDonald, R Ferguson, G Stuart; third row: William Wilson, Brian Davidson, Eileen Mackenzie, Elizabeth Corbett, Cathie Ann MacNeil, A Anderson, K Beck, A Fenton; second row: Margaret Yeudall, Jean Smith, E Mackay Norma Reid, Mary Urquhart, M Watson, A Watson, Carol Garrioch; front row – John Maclennan, C MacRae, Hector Munro (head boy), Lorna Fraser (head girl), Maureen Balfour, Bernice Sheehan. Eileen Mackenzie, who identified most of the group, recalls: "Calum Macdonald was from Skye, Ronnie Mackenzie and John Maclennan were from Harris and Cathie Ann MacNeil was from Barra. Brian Davidson was a very good swimmer."

Former pupils of a certain age will recognise their teachers of yesteryear in this photo of Inverness High School staff from 1960.

This photo features a group of Inverness Technical High School pupils modelling outfits made at sewing classes during session 1952-53. Marjorie Sutherland, now Stuart, who submitted the picture, is on the extreme left of the fourth row. She says: "Others in the photo are Kay MacKenzie, Maureen Ness and Louise Ross, but I have forgotten the names of most of the others." The lone lucky man is the art teacher, whose name, Marjorie thinks, was Derek Ashby.

We can only identify one person from this class from Central School of 1922-23. Christina Matheson is the cheery looking wee girl fourth from the left in the rear row. Her cousin John Matheson succeeded his father as office manager of the Inverness Courier in the 1960s.

Merkinch Primary School Choir pictured in the mid-1960s. Does anybody remember the occasion?

Another Merkinch Primary School photo of older pupils from 1966 – rear from left: Maria Schurie, Alexis Cormie, Glynne MacDonald, Eleanor Ross, Margaret Wood; third row, from left: Sandra Allan, Brenda Johnstone, Mary Murchison, Sheila Fraser, Sandra Allan, Sylvia Clark, Louise Skinner, Linda Clelland, Deirdre Mackay; second row, from left: Donna Falconer, Hazel Ross, Kathleen Aitken, Heather Campbell, Marie MacKenzie, Glynis Macrae, Sharon Clark Heather Macdonald; front, from left: Joseph MacKenzie, William Junor, George Junor.

This happy group from Merkinch Primary School was pictured at Inverness railway station prior to leaving on the first stage of an exciting trip on the schools cruise ship SS Dunera Castle. In the photo, rear row, from left, are: Sandra Allan (B), David Shaw, Graham Gordon, Sylvia Clark, Colin Paulin, Hamish McConnachie. Front row, from left: Pat Fraser; Louise Skinner, Sheila Fraser, Mary Murchison, Eileen Wheeler, Sandra Allan (A)

On the threshold of higher education or a career in June 1947 were these members of Form 6B, Inverness Royal Academy. In the back row from left are: Peter Chisholm, Billy Irvine, St Clair "Patchy" Calder, Jock MacDougall, Andy Mackintosh, Harold "Balder" Beaton, "Spiv" Bethune, Derrick MacKenzie; front: Elspeth Campbell, Fiona Fraser, Gladys MacLennon, English teacher Eva MacKenzie, Alison MacNair, Margaret Corbett, Ella Graham.

Inverness Technical High School sixth year of 1954 – Rear row, from left: John Macleod, Wullie Mackintosh, Donald Munro, Arthur Murray, James Clark, Albert Jeans; third row: Walter Cumming, Calum Macleod, Donald Bowker, Peter Douglas, Donald Matheson; second row: Iris Beaton, Chrissie Fraser, Betty Graham, Margaret Thompson, Rhoda Macleod, Bella MacNeil, unidentified, Madeline Sutherland, Rosa Storey, Betty Murray; front: Jean MacRae (vice-captain), Bob Aitken (captain), lady superintendent Isobel Swanston, headmaster William G Johnston, Mr Beaton, Winifred Gaston (captain), Ramsay Aitken (vice-captain).

Senior pupils pictured at Inverness Royal Academy sports day in June 1948. In the back row, from left, are: "Twin" Dunbar, "Thaitch" MacKenzie, Louis Forrai, Gordon Goulder, Billy Irvine, Ian MacDonald, Elspeth Campbell, Betty Lauder, Peter Chisholm, "Spiv" Bethune; front: "Peem" Munro, Belle Munro, Margaret Corbett, Alison MacNair, Martin Forrai.

Central Primary School senior pupils circa 1947. In the picture are, rear row, from left: B Murray, Adam Grant, J Thompson, R Fraser, L Grant, Christopher Fraser, P Douglas, Murdo MacKenzie, I MacKenzie, Ali Urquhart; mid row, from left: A Paterson, E Melrose, P Cummings, J Reid, P MacDonald, M MacDonald, M Baird, C Clark, S MacLennan, Colin McHardy, Ali Chisholm; front, from left, C Innes, M Mackay, M Boag, G Mackay, I Beaton, E Finlay, M Smith, E Gunn, J Ross, I Ross, Marjorie MacKenzie, Rosemary Maxwell.

More about a local celebrity

In Inverness Remembered V we featured Inverness gym teacher, strong-man, heavyweight athlete, actor, comedian, entertainer and singer, Donald Dallas, better known locally as Donal, Don or Dan.

Born in 1875, Dan was one of the Highland Capital's great characters of the late Victorian era and early 20th Century. Remembered as much for his majestic nose as for his superb physique, Dan was only 5ft 5in tall, but regularly outperformed much taller rivals on the sports circuit.

We asked if any of our readers remembered the year of his death and received a swift response, together with some more photos, from a young kinsman, Jamie Angus.

Says Jamie: "He died in Inverness in December 1946 and is buried with his wife Jessie in Tomnahurich Cemetery. As well as being a 'physical culture expert', he was a moderately successful folk singer and old 78 rpm records of his recordings are quite collectible today.

"He was the fifth child of Alexander Dallas, a prominent figure in Inverness in the late 19th century, who owned a jeweller's and watchmaker's shop in Church Street and was also an optician and a keen photographer.

"Alexander's photo appears in page 6 of Volume 3 of Inverness Remembered. He died in 1906. Alexander's father was Peter Dallas, who was one half of Dallas & Mackintosh, an Inverness painting firm which existed up until at least the 1860s. I am descended from Peter through his son John Dallas. One of Alexander's other sons, I think James, founded Dallas's the Jewellers in Nairn which still exists today, albeit under different management. At one time the family lived at 4 Hill Place, Inverness.

"Alexander was himself a direct ancestor of William Dallas who was a prominent merchant in Inverness in the 17th century. William's accounts book still survives and certainly until recently could still be viewed in the Highland Archives. From William, it is possible to trace the Dallas line back centuries."

While researching the Dallas family tree, Jamie has been in correspondence with a kinsman Evan Dallas in America, a descendant of Alexander Dallas the watchmaker.

Dan Dallas, in comic pose,
with his wife Jessie and their two daughters.

Dan Dallas in 1932, when he was still a very fit 57.

Dan Dallas in his youth, already extremely muscular and superbly fit. The famous "nose that launched a thousand quips" does not seem quite so prominent as it was in later years.

Dan Dallas with his wife Jessie and unidentified members of his family, two of whom are thought to be his daughters..

Growing up in Inverness

Alan Simmons was born in Hamilton, Lanarkshire, but moved to Inverness in 1935 as a toddler, when his father William, a native of Manchester, was promoted manager of Timpson's shoe shop, then at 48 High Street.

Alan spent his formative years in the Highland Capital, until he left Inverness Royal Academy in 1950.

He moved to Edinburgh following his father's promotion to area manager there, and began a 23-year spell with Timpson's, punctuated by National Service as a jet fighter pilot in the RAF.

Alan, who retired north in 2007, having maintained his connections with Inverness throughout his life, and having himself being widowed, married the widow of one of his close school friends, the late Lewis Nairn.

Despite his English ancestry, he regards himself as a Highlander and a Scotsman, and retains fond memories of the Inverness of his youth and his old school.

A family at war – The war was still on when this photo was taken outside the Simmons' family home at 4 Holm Avenue, as schoolboy Alan was carrying his gasmask. The trio in the picture are his maternal grandparents on holiday from Manchester, Albert and Alice Clarke, and his mother Alice. Note the pile of bricks, assembled ready to build an air-raid shelter if need be.

76 Dores beach is not very different today from what it was when this photo was taken in 1936. Toddler Alan is supported on the gunwale of the boat by his mother Alice.

When this photo was taken at Rosemarkie in September 1936, Alan Simmons was only two and a half years old. "No swings now, otherwise just the same," he says.

Alan Simmons' English relatives pictured around 1950 in the course of a tour in a bus owned by Inverness motor concern MacRae & Dick, which then also supplied a variety of vehicles for hire or public service. The bus, one of a small fleet operated by the company to provide tours and scheduled services, is possibly a 1936 Albion Victor. MacRae & Dick sold its buses to Highland Omnibuses Ltd in 1952. Alan thinks the photo was taken at Inverfarigaig.

A rural scene in Glenurquhart Road, circa 1936. Is the man on the bicycle herding the cattle along, or is he merely waiting to pass?

Alan Simmons enjoys the experience of using the rare "bucket bridge" across the River Findhorn at Pollachaig, along with his grandparents Albert and Alice Clarke, circa 1938.

Rosemarkie beach around 1936. Note that despite the relaxed mood of the photo, both men are both quite formally attired, the elder, Albert Clarke, wearing a suit, the younger, his son-in-law William Simmons, a smart sports jacket and flannels, while each wears a tie. Between them is Alice Simmons, William's wife.

Family on the swings at Nairn around 1938 – from left: Alice Simmons, Alice Clarke, Alan Simmons, Albert Clarke.

Civic service

The centuries-old Inverness Town Council was finally disbanded in 1975, in the wake of a two-tier Scottish local government reorganisation featuring new regional and district councils.

This experiment proved somewhat too bureaucratic and top-heavy, with the two-tier system itself abolished in favour of a unitary council system in 1996.

The office of provost lives on, however, a prominent local Highland councillor being voted in as such today by his peers from the area.

Local businessman and former provost Ian Fraser, who held the burgh's leading role for five years from 1975, as the first head of Inverness District Council, after some years as member and bailie on Inverness Town Council, provided most of these photographs.

The first picture, however, comes from reader Marjorie Stuart. Stepping out from the railway station, HM Queen Elizabeth is welcomed to Inverness by Lord Lieutenant, Boer War and Great War veteran Sir Donald Walter Cameron KT, 25th chief of Clan Cameron, left, and Provost Hugh Ross, while the tall, erect man of Hollywood hearthrob appearance, walking behind, is World War II hero and commando leader, the late Lord Lovat, reputedly described by Prime Minister Winston Churchill as "the handsomest man who ever slit a throat". The photo is thought to have been taken prior to the opening of the Highland Show in 1948, at which both King George VI and the Queen were present. In that year the King bestowed the show, which then alternated between a number of larger Northern Scottish towns, before being hijacked permanently by Ingliston, Edinburgh, in 1960, with the Royal accolade. Provost Ross held office from 1945-49. Sir Donald Cameron, born in 1876, died in October 1951. As the recently widowed Queen Mother, Queen Elizabeth received the Freedom of Inverness in 1953.

The second photo was passed on by Margaret Gordon, whose father, the late Jimmy Sinclair, a director of A I Welders Ltd, was then the burgh treasurer. It features members of the Town Council, pictured in the council chamber just after the 1967 local election, with at their head, new Provost William A Smith, who was to serve until 1975, when the town council was disbanded and succeeded by the short-lived Inverness District Council. The members, from bottom left, clockwise, are Douglas Baxter, Tom MacKenzie, Robbie Grigor, Stuart MacLennan, Kenneth MacLeod, Hamish Gray, Bill Fraser, Mario Bernardi, Provost Smith, John MacDonald, Jackie Fraser, Jimmy Sinclair, Adam Grant, Neil Godsman, Jimmy Still, Jim Cameron, Bob King, William "Dan" Urquhart, Helen Kennedy, Tom Smith, Alistair Milne. The officials around the lower table, are, from left, Derek Bigg, John R Hill, Douglas Mollison and Jock Will. The only currently serving councillor of this intake at time of publication is Ken MacLeod, elected to Highland Council in 2007, after many years' absence from local politics.

Provost Smith was still civic head when this picture was taken four years later, but several new faces had by then appeared, and the top civic roles had changed. At the top table, beside council officer Charlie Macrae (standing) are from left: Ritchie McPhee, Peter Drummond, Alastair Milne, the Rev Ian McIntosh, minister of the Old High Church, Provost William A Smith, Ian Fraser, Margaret Fraser, Bill Fraser; middle table, from left: finance director Derek Bigg, Dan Corbett, Mabel Skinner, town clerk John R Hill; main table, clockwise from nearest: Mario Bernardi, - Murray, Gerald Pollitt, Hamish Beauchop, Tom MacKenzie, Allan Sellar, Hamish Sutherland, Gordon Campbell, Hector MacDonald, Annie Rodgers, Jimmy Cameron, Ron Lyon.

This photo, taken on the stairway of the Town House, may well be of members of an authority in transition from a town council to a district council, in the mid-1970s.

William A Smith was still provost, in the dying years of Inverness Town Council, when the Queen Mother made one of her many visits to the burgh in the early 1970s. When this photo was taken in the foyer of the Station Hotel, she was chatting up popular local MP Russell Johnston – later Sir Russell and eventually raised to the peerage. With Mr Johnston are his wife Joan, while on the left is Bailie Ian Fraser, later to become the new district authority's first provost. The Queen Mother was proud of her status as Freeman of the Burgh, conferred in 1953, and made a point of wearing her freeman's ring on several subsequent visits.

Provost Ian Fraser steps out in the forefront of a Christian Aid sponsored walk, snapped in Ardross Street in the late 1970s.

The late Jimmy Nairn receives a plaque from Inverness Provost Ian Fraser in recognition of his contribution to the burgh, to which he came in 1941, as manager of the Playhouse Cinema. He is best remembered by those of a certain age for the way in which he turned the Playhouse café into a festive-season wonderland, with Disney characters painted by himself and members of his family. When the Playhouse burned down in 1972, he continued the festive theme in his own home in Lochardil for a number of years, and invited local children round to enjoy its wonders. This picture from the 1970s, with his wife Mary and some of his grandchildren and neighbours, must have been taken around Christmas time.

Farewell to a landmark city church

A fine late spring day in May 2010 heralded the end of an era in the ecclesiastical life of Inverness. On the 9th of that month, St Columba High Church in the city's Bank Street, closed after a poignant farewell service, its falling congregational roll having succeeded in bringing about what a near-disastrous fire had failed to do in war's darkest days, 70 years before.

It was almost immediately put up for sale by Church of Scotland headquarters in Edinburgh, along with its associated Dr Black Memorial Halls.

The St Columba High congregation, originally known as the English Free Church to emphasise the language of worship, dates from the Disruption which split the Established Church of Scotland in 1843.

The present building, by MacKenzie and Matthews in perpendicular Gothic style, dates from 1852, and includes a splendid rose window above the chancel, installed in the 1950s to replace an earlier, similar fire-damaged window.

The congregation later seceded from the Free Church to join the United Free Church, the bulk of which rejoined the Established Church in 1929, to form the present Church of Scotland.

The present building was heavily damaged by fire in May 1940, as Hitler's Nazis were invading the Low Countries and France, and only weeks before thousands of young men from Inverness and the Highlands were captured with the 51st Highland Division at St Valery.

However, it was rebuilt by the voluntary work of members of the congregation, using "tip-up" cinema style-seating, a legacy perhaps of the fact that it held its services in the former La Scala Cinema until it reopened in 1948. Timber for the roofing was found by using salvaged rafters from the fire, supplemented by Russian timber and wood from crates of Oregon pine in which American aircraft had been shipped to Britain during the war.

A photographic record of the life of the church was compiled in 1970-71 when the Rev Stephen Frew was minister.

Following closure, enthusiasts took a last opportunity to photograph the church and halls interiors, as these are expected to disappear in their present form when the buildings are sold.

The halls, which cost £2000 to build, and opened in 1907, were named after Rev John J Black, a former minister of the congregation. Following the union of 1929, the hall became the regular meeting place of the reformed Presbytery of Inverness, and was also used by several other religious and secular bodies. The presbytery continued to meet there until mid-2010.

Despite the town-centre church's closure, the name will live on as St Columba New Charge, a reconstituted congregation based in a new, as yet to be built church, in a southern suburb of the city.

Photographed outside Dr Black Memorial Halls in Bank Street in October 1929 were these formally-attired reverend gentlemen and elders of Inverness Church of Scotland Presbytery, which even then had started to meet in that fine building, completed 22 years earlier, as an adjunct to the nearby St Columba High Church at a cost of £2,000. That year was particularly significant in Scottish clerical history, as the date the bulk of the former breakaway United Free Church, including the St Columba congregation, reunited with the Established Church of Scotland to form the present organisation. How different in appearance are these worthy men of yesteryear from the ministers and elders of today, although their attitudes and aims may not have deviated very much. Today's presbytery members, who until 2010 attended meetings at the Dr Black Halls, are generally much more casually dressed – while many, unlike those in the photo, are now women.

Mr Campbell, Ex-Provost K. Macrae, J.P., Rev. G. McWilliam, B.D., Rev. E. J. F. Elliot, Mr A. McHattie.

Mr C. Clark, Rev. Alex. Boyd, M.A., Mr J. McPherson, Bailie A. Smith,   Rev. J. B. MacArthur, Mr A. W. Fraser, Rev. D. Macgillivray, B.D., Rev. N. Maclellan, Mr A. P. W. Bewglass, Rev. J. Macleod, M.A., Mr Blackhall, Mr D. Grant, Mr D. Macdonald, Mr D. Ross, Mr D. Fraser, Mr J. Young.

Mr Ross, Mr D. Maclennan, Rev. Stewart Mechie, M.A., Mr J. Farquhar, Mr A. Mowat, Mr D. Mackintosh, Rev. R. L. Wiseman, Mr A. Kennedy, Rev. W. Metcalfe, B.D., Rev. W. King, B.D., Rev. J. Ross, M.A., Mr J. H. Davidson, Rev. D. Macleod, B.D., M.C., Rev. W. Sutherland, Mr S. Service, Rev. A. Hamilton, B.D., Rev. D. Macdonald, Rev. J. MacCallum, Rev. N. Mackenzie, M.A., Mr Elliot Ross, Rev. D. G. Brook, M.C., Mr A. Mackenzie, Mr J. Macbean, Mr P. Campbell, Rev. J. Morton, M.A.

Ex-Provost Petrie, J.P., Mr T. McEwan, O.B.E., M.V.D. Mr W. McMillan, Rev. A. J. Macdonald, M.A., Mr A. Robertson, S.S.C., Rev. C. Fraser, B.D., Rev. W. M. Graham, M.A., Rev. A. Maclean, B.D., Rev. J. Tolmie, M.A., Rev. W. R. Pirrie, D.D., Rev. K. Maclean, Rev. J. Wright, M.A., Rev. A. MacIver, Rev. A. M. Macfarlane, Rev. Angus Boyd, M.A., Mr W. Law, Mr J. Maclean, Mr W. L. MacWilliam.

The names of the ministers and elders at the October 1929 meeting.

Contrast these Sunday school youngsters from the 1940s, snapped at an outing to Nairn, with those of nearly three decades later.

St Columba High Church after the disastrous fire of May 1940, before the roof collapsed.

Pictured here with leader Eileen Livingstone are members of St Columba High 12th Brownies of 1969-70. Where are these young ladies now?

St Columba High's Sunday School was thriving when this photo was taken in 1971.

When this photo of St Columba High Church congregation was taken in 1971, numbers were still quite substantial. Sadly the passage of nearly four decades has taken its toll on membership, and with too few replacing those who have passed on, the church closed on 9 May 2010 after a last poignant service. The name will live on as St Columba New Charge in a reconstituted congregation based in a southern suburb of the city.

Some members of St Columba High choir meet in the vestry in 1971 with minister the Rev Stephen Frew.

Pictured at his console in 1971 was St Columba High Church organist the late David Hardie, a talented local musician, who sadly died at an early age.

A Christian Aid sponsored walk in 1969 turning into Ness Bank from the Ness Bridge. Prominent in the midst, in his white raincoat, is Provost William Smith, a Great War veteran and businessman, not to be confused with his 21st Century civic namesake of the same name.

Repairs taking place to St Columba High steeple nearly 40 years ago.

St Columba High Church Woman's Guild photographed celebrating the 50th anniversary of its foundation on 27 Feb 1990. The photograph was taken by Allan Beattie, and the lady fourth left in the front row is Mrs Elizabeth Frew, wife of former minister Rev Stephen Frew, who was invited to join the Guild on this occasion.

Forces memories

Alex Fridge, now 75 and living in Wellington, New Zealand, last year sent us some photos, three of which we published in Inverness Remembered V. Here are a couple, which didn't make the last issue, of Alex in uniform. Alex, who still regards himself as a true Merkincher, born in "The Ferry", has had a number of jobs, including being a member of the NZ Diplomatic Protection Squad for some years.

A teenage Alex Fridge poses around 1950, while attending annual camp at Crail, Fife, in the uniform of the Queen's Own Cameron Highlanders Army Cadet Force, when he was bass drummer of Inverness Army Cadet Pipe Band.

Three years later Private Alex Fridge is photographed shouldering a .303 Mk IV Lee-Enfield army rifle during his second week of National Service training at Farnborough, Hants, in the uniform of the Royal Army Service Corps. He is wearing the standard issue 37 Pattern battledress, introduced in 1937, and still in use by Territorial Army units in the mid-1960. By the end of his service he was sporting a corporal's two stripes, as his photo in Inverness Remembered V showed.

Territorial Army soldier lassies circa 1960, in front of an early LandRover, when Inverness still boasted a number of different part-time army units. The three from the left are Peggy Royce, Eirwen Mellis and Ann Grant. The others are unidentified.

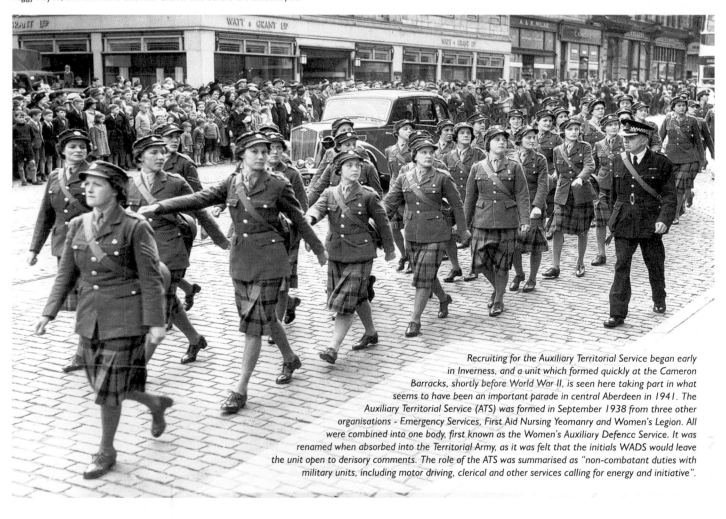

Recruiting for the Auxiliary Territorial Service began early in Inverness, and a unit which formed quickly at the Cameron Barracks, shortly before World War II, is seen here taking part in what seems to have been an important parade in central Aberdeen in 1941. The Auxiliary Territorial Service (ATS) was formed in September 1938 from three other organisations - Emergency Services, First Aid Nursing Yeomanry and Women's Legion. All were combined into one body, first known as the Women's Auxiliary Defence Service. It was renamed when absorbed into the Territorial Army, as it was felt that the initials WADS would leave the unit open to derisory comments. The role of the ATS was summarised as "non-combatant duties with military units, including motor driving, clerical and other services calling for energy and initiative".

Members of Inverness ATS unit warrant officers' and sergeants' mess pictured at Craigmonie, now Craigmonie Hotel, in July 1940, when the Battle of Britain was approaching its height. Sergeant Christina Matheson, to whom this picture belonged, is third from the left in the second row. The next picture is of the members' autographs on the back of the photo.

This picture shows the autographs, on the back of the previous photo, of the warrant officers and sergeants of Inverness unit of the Auxiliary Territorial Service, based at Cameron Barracks and billeted in what is now the Craigmonie Hotel.

These smart Territorial Army soldiers from Inverness-based Headquarters Company, 4/5th Battalion Queen's Own Cameron Highlanders, were photographed at camp in Scarborough in June 1954. Peter Chisholm, who submitted this picture, is third from the right in the middle row. He also identified colleague Hugh Williamson as second from the right in the rear row. Note the World War II campaign medals worn proudly by some of the more senior members of the company. Sadly that fine regiment, which so successfully resisted Napoleon, the Kaiser and Hitler, has long since marched into history, the victims of Britain's political classes, in the name of expediency and economy, the 1st Camerons having amalgamated with the 1st Seaforth Highlanders in 1961, to form the 1st Queen's Own Highlanders. The 4/5th Battalion survived in its original form until a major reorganisation of the TA in 1967. A remnant of Cameron history survives today in the blue hackle worn by 4th (Highlanders) Battalion, Royal Regiment of Scotland, but the Erracht Cameron tartan has long since vanished from the parade ground.

This quartet formed part of the Inverness Sea Cadet Corps guard for the opening of TS Citadel, at Inverness Longman, in August 1946. At the rear, from left are Cadets Peter Chisholm and Len Fraser, in front P Gibson and David Morris. The original Inverness Sea Cadet unit was founded in 1942, at the height of World War II, based at first in Central School. In 1946, when this photo was taken the base moved close to the Longman site where Cromwell's Citadel had stood, which gave the unit the name TS Citadel. In the late 1950s the cadets had to relocate when BP wanted to expand its neighbouring fuel depot. They were given a site at the former Kessock Farm, just across the harbour, where they remain today. After the move the unit changed its name to TS Briton after the former Royal Naval Reserve drill ship HMS Briton, moored in the Caledonian Canal's Muirtown Basin for many years until broken up in 1908. The letters TS stand for Training Ship.

Relaxation, nights out and entertainment

Drumossie Hotel staff forget about their hard work for a few hours and enjoy themselves at their staff dance, pictured here some time in the 1960s.

A presentation at the Station Hotel in the early 1970s. The tall young recipient is thought to be a junior chef who was leaving to go to Gleneagles Hotel, and the man making the presentation Mr Cameron, head chef. The lady with the bouquet is thought to be Mrs Cameron.

Another Station Hotel presentation from the 1970s. The man making it is Louis Martin, at that time the hotel's general manager.

Pictured here are members of the Station Hotel staff in the 1970s, at what seems to be a presentation ceremony. The lady with the bouquet is thought to be Mrs Cameron, wife of head chef Mr Cameron, beside her, and the man at the right in the front row is general manager Louis Martin. Peggy Fraser, to whom the photo belongs, is second from the left in the front row, with beside her Erna Eckhart. In the second row from the bottom, far left, is former local shopkeeper and burgh bailie Mario Bernardi, who supplied the hotel with vegetables. Third from the left in the same row is bar manager Robbie Van Reenan, who presided over his famous Robbie's Bar in the hotel for many years.

Another photograph of Station Hotel staff enjoying themselves, this time at the Caledonian Hotel. Peggy Fraser is front row, left, and Margaret Mackillop, front right.

Happy revellers at Inverness Motor Company's annual dance, snapped in February 1973.

The Heatherlea Band was a popular group in the burgh in the 1960s. Pictured here in its heyday in 1965, are from left : Tommy Cameron, Jeannie Kennedy, Billy Plowman, Dan Mackenzie, Jock Fraser.

Allan Cameron receives a watch from colleague and long time friend Roy Reid, on his retirement in 1969, after serving 46 years with the Gas Board. He started as a meter inspector and retired as a commercial assistant in the board office in Union Street, now occupied by Jessops. On Allan's other side is Gas Board manager John Ford, while the lady with the bouquet is Allan's wife, Bella (nee Shand). Outwith his employment, Allan was a well-known local actor and comedian, who performed in many venues around the town, including the Catch my Pal Hall in Academy Street and the sadly-demolished Empire Theatre. He acted in many amateur dramas and produced and directed for the Queen's Own Cameron Highlanders War Memorial Boys' Club drama group and St Michael's Drama Club. He also had a part in a 1939 film, Power to the Highlands.

Employees, partners and friends pictured at the staff dance of postcard manufacturer J Arthur Dixon, January 1960. The Isle of Wight-based company, founded by talented Yorkshire-born printer and photographer John Arthur Dixon, opened its Highland satellite in May 1956, in one of the early purpose-built factories in the Longman Industrial Estate. It flourished successfully until the late 1970s, when the company experienced financial difficulties. The building, which was sold to Stratton's Dairies, was demolished in 2004 to make way for a new development.

It's gala day at Inverness Thistle Park in the early 1950s, and this charming fancy dress picture appears to depict a Wild West wedding. The bride and bridesmaids are obvious, but which, if any of the cast, is the groom.

This quintet of Highland dancers, from Edith Macpherson's famous dancing school, were pictured in June 1960, although we've not been told the occasion. The girls second and third from the left, respectively, are named as Sheila Mackintosh and Ruby Ross, while the lass on the extreme right is Jackie Sinclair. Can any of our readers identify the other two?

There were smiles all round when these members of Inverness Baptist Church held their Christmas party in 1956 in the since long-demolished Albert Hotel in Eastgate. In the centre of the picture are minister the Rev John MacBeath and his wife.

Inverness Courier staff and partners gather in the new Caledonian Hotel in 1967 to hold a 150th anniversary dinner, hosted by the autocratic Miss Eveline Barron OBE MA, editor and proprietor, as she was always described. Despite her somewhat adversarial attitude, her very definite and often outspoken views on a huge range of subjects, Miss Barron had a reputation for being courteous and kind to her staff. Among those visible at Table 7 are Lesley Macpherson, Grant Henderson, Marilyn Inch, Lorna Skinner, and George, while those identified at Table 8 include Alan Forsyth, Alex MacAskill, Ann Wemyss, John Hart, Ian Williams, Mrs Rhind, Tommy Rhind, Mrs J MacKenzie, Mrs Roy Livingstone, Reg, Bobby, Richard, John Graham, David Rennie, Donnie, Veronica Blande, Bob and wife, Roy Livingstone.

A neighbours' get-together in Smith Avenue circa 1960. Seated, left, on a settee arm, is Cissie Dickson, with beside her Annie Mellis. In the middle is an unidentified boy, while along from him are a Mrs Steen and John MacDonald. Standing, behind, are May MacDonald, two unidentified, Mrs and Mr Dickson and engine driver Jimmy MacDonald.

This Christmas party picture was taken at the Haugh around 1960. Linda Law, then Linda Mellis, who submitted it, is in the third row from the front, second from the left. The party, she tells us, was organised by the Eastern Star Ladies, including Lizzie Ross, from Smith Avenue, while she names other youngsters in the photo as Norman and Ronnie Sutherland and Pat Laing.

Members of Inverness Townswomen's Guild gather for a social evening and supper at the former Methodist Church in the 1950s.

Revellers at A I Welders' annual dance in 1959, pictured at a time when the pioneering Inverness firm was still exporting state-of-the-art rail welding machines across the world. It appears to have been rather a grand affair, with nearly all of the men wearing evening dress and bow ties. The man in the kilt in the front row is the late Major Pat Hunter Gordon, who had taken over as company chairman shortly before from his father Sam Hunter Gordon. Major Pat, who had won a Military Cross for gallantry in World War II was made CBE for his services to industry in 1976, but died sadly in a motor accident when campaigning as prospective Conservative candidate for Inverness-shire shortly before the 1979 General Election. Beside him are his mother and wife Valerie. Front, third from left is James Sinclair, whose pioneering work on PLUTO, the ingenious pipeline under the ocean which pumped millions of gallons of petrol across the Channel for invading forces in Europe after D-Day, was rewarded with an MBE. It was modest enough recompense for masterminding a development which dispensed with the need for large numbers of vulnerable tankers and manpower, and doubtless helped to save many lives. Extreme left, front row, is Bill Young, with Bessie Sinclair between him and her husband. Second from the right, front row, is William H Millwood.

Enjoying themselves at their annual dance, around 1956, were these members of British Rail's Inverness clerical staff and friends. Among those present was district superintendent Alan Yeaman, a well known local Justice of the Peace who held a number of other important positions in the burgh.

This photo of the leading members of A I Welders at the company's dinner-dance in the early 1950s was taken by Sandy McLaren, who ran the Inverness branch of his Perth-based family firm, Star Photos, for many years from the early 1930s. As an official war photographer Sandy took many dramatic action pictures during the Western Desert campaign. Second from the right, front, wearing a kilt, is Sam Hunter Gordon, whose vision and enterprise developed A I Welders from a small provincial iron foundry to a world leader in the manufacture of resistance-welding equipment.

Inverness Round Table members from the 1960s pictured with president Hector MacVinish, front, centre.

These youngsters of Inverness Methodist Church were enjoying their Sunday School party in the former church in Union Street, in the austerity wartime days of the early 1940s. Isobel Henry, nee Macdonald, who submitted the picture, is the sixth girl from the left in the fifth row from the front, wearing a paper crown, while her brother Tommy is the wee boy fourth row from the front, on the extreme right.

The well-known Inverness Florians drama group, pictured taking a break from a costume drama in the 1950s. In the picture, are rear, from left, two unidentified members, Sandy Halley and John Innes; front Pat Gulley, now Mrs Smith, who submitted this photo, Laura MacDonald, Annabel Ward and Peggy Angus.

The Florians again, on stage, in a production depicting the 19th Century, dating also from the 1950s. The players here are, standing from left: Pat Gulley, unidentified, unidentified, Gordon Crawford, Annabel Ward, unidentified, unidentified, Ivor Humphries; seated, Isa Fowler. The group, which still flourishes in the city, was founded in 1944 to entertain troops stationed in the area.

This cheery group was snapped at Queensgate Electrical's staff dance in the early 1950s. The stamp on the back, Star Photos, Commercial Photographers, 75 Kinnoull Street, Perth, indicates that is was taken by the late Sandy Mclaren, who set up a branch office of his family's photographic business in Inverness in the early 1930s. Sandy served as a captain in the Black Watch during World War II eventually becoming an official army photographer. He took many pictures of the late General Bernard Montgomery and of the 8th Army in action in the desert, until he was wounded and invalided out of active service. He returned to Inverness on demob, but shortly after this photo was taken, bachelor Sandy went back to his native town on his father's retirement from the main branch. He frequently visited Inverness until shortly before his death in the 1990s, and bequeathed many of his negatives to Inverness branch of the Royal British Legion.

This photo, of members of Inverness County Badminton Team in the 1950s is included in our nights out section as they were obviously in party rather than playing mode, though the rim of a trophy is just visible at the bottom. Rear, from left: I MacLeod, I Munro, N Munro, B Mann, A McCutcheon, H MacEwan, M Smith; middle row, from left: F Lawson, W MacKenzie, N Mann, M MacEwan, B Fraser, E MacKenzie; front, from left, unidentified, unidentified, P Gulley, D Cameron.

A Clan Fraser gathering at Beaufort Castle circa 1969. Second from the right is Lovat Fraser chief and war hero, Simon Fraser, Lord Lovat, with beside him wartime Lovat Scouts' piper and renowned fiddler, Pipe Major Donald Riddell, Kirkhill.

Inverness Girls' Choir, pictured in the early 1950s with conductor Elizabeth Haldane and pianist Bud Sutherland.

Members of Inverness Townswomen's Guild, pictured at a meeting in the Cummings Hotel in 1969.

Pictured on the stairs of the since demolished La Scala Cinema in Strothers Lane in 1997 was this happy group. Can any reader identify the occasion and the people in the photo?

Staff of Mackay's Bookshop in High Street, by then owned by John Menzies, enjoy a night out at the Columba Hotel in 1952. This photo was submitted by Irene MacPherson, then Mackay, seated fourth from the right. Her boss, Mr Beveridge, wearing a bow tie, is fourth from the left in the same row.

Miscellania from bygone days

At the Bucht, Inverness

A picture from around the turn of last century of "The Bucht" – note the old spelling of The Bught – taken close to the bridge to Whin Island. It comes from a postcard sent on 1st February 1919 to a Mrs A West, of Brackley, Northamptonshire, by a man "on active service" who signs himself Alf, and addresses her as "Dear H." He continues: "Got your two letters late last night and was so glad to hear that you was well and glad that N is better and quite well." He adds: "We arrived at Chatham today and I think dear that I shall be home by the middle of next week." Was Alf a sailor, writing to his wife on a postcard he had bought when his ship had called in at Inverness? The Great War had by that time been over for nearly three months, but the Royal Navy, which had a major base at Chatham, Kent, was still very busily engaged in watching the German Fleet, by then interned at Scapa Flow, and more urgently perhaps in the hazardous task of clearing huge minefields in the North Sea. Was it possible that H and N were recovering from that other scourge of the 20th Century's second decade, the Spanish 'flu epidemic, which claimed more victims among service personnel and civilians across Europe than the war itself?

"Dig this for a pram," writes Anne C MacKintosh, who submitted this photo of her brother Murdo MacKenzie, taken when he was only a few months old in 1936.

93

Inverness mother Chrissie MacKenzie on a shopping trip in the burgh's High Street in 1954, with her daughter Anne, who submitted this photo. The wee lad with his back to the camera seems to be wearing school uniform – perhaps he was making his way back to Inverness Royal Academy, then at the top of Stephen's Brae. And doesn't the rather formidable looking lady on the right look just like a schoolteacher of that era?

Inverness. A Walk at Ness Islands.

A study of the Ness Islands in the late Victorian or Edwardian era, from a contemporary postcard. Perhaps a reader with some expertise in fashions of yesteryear might be able to place the period more accurately.

These music enthusiasts were holding a sale in aid of funds for Inverness Folk Festival 1987.

A relatively youthful Queen Elizabeth meets local Girl Guides at the Northern Meeting Park around 1960, during a visit to Inverness. She is pictured here talking to Jackie Sinclair, who later became a leading enthusiast in the Inverness folk song scene, and retired recently from a long career in the city library.

All we know about this photo is that it was taken in October 1957 at the Clachnaharry Inn, and features Walter Innes (left), his wife Jean and friend George "Butch" Sinclair.

Princesses were fabulous females from story books or fairy tales to six-year old Lynn Jarvis, until the day in 1977 when she met and talked to a real live princess. Lynn, whose dad, the late Tim Jarvis, was then a member of the Junior Chamber Committee which organised the grand finale of the International Gathering of the Clans, enjoyed the privilege of presenting a bouquet to the guest of honour, Princess Alexandra, in her heyday one of the most popular Royals, if not one of the most highly paid.

Princess Alexandra is pictured here again in 1984 being greeted by Lord Lieutenant Sir Donald Cameron of Lochiel as she arrives to open the new Smithton Youth Centre in October 1984. The police driver in the photo is Constable Jimmy Sutherland, while in the background, wearing his customary pork-pie hat, is Chief Constable Donald Henderson.

A birthday party group taken in Lochalsh Road in the 1960s. Mary Nicoll, who submitted it, says: "I can't identify all the children involved, but David and Gordon Straube, Robert Bruce, Hamish McConnachie, the Bain children and Mary Murchison are in the photograph."

The adventurous little lass in this charming late 1930s photo is Christine Shivas. She's standing boldly on the old German field howitzer, a trophy from the Great War, which stood outside Inverness Castle front door for many years after the conflict. Christine, later Mackenzie, was born in 1934 and died in 2008. Her sister Pat Munro, now living in Elgin, submitted the picture. The field gun, captured at Loos in 1915 by the Queen's Own Cameron Highlanders, was later moved to the entrance hall inside the castle. It is now at the Clan Cameron Museum at Achnacarry Castle, Lochaber, where clan chief the late Colonel Sir Donald Cameron offered it refuge over 40 years ago when the authorities sought to dispose of it.

Helen Finlayson, of Scorguie Drive, Inverness, who submitted this old picture of lady pierrots would love to know who the members of this winsome foursome were. They were obviously taking part in a play, show or tableau of the sort popular in the burgh in the early part of last century. The photo, taken by D Whyte's studio in Church Street, Inverness, came from the home of her grandparents, whose family name was Fox, but she adds: "We know for sure it is not any of the Fox family of this generation, who now are all nearly 80 years old." A handwritten note on the back of the photo, printed as a postcard, states that the girl front left could be Dolly Mackinnon, wife of Thomas Fox. Can any reader help Mrs Finlayson find any more about the participants?

Queen Victoria still had a substantial part of her reign in front of her when this photo of Jessie Snowie and her family was taken, about 1885, at the then popular local studio of MacMahon. Jessie's husband Tom and his father at that time ran the successful business of Hugh Snowie, taxidermists and gunsmiths, in Church Street, approximately where Asher's bakery stands today. Tom was a burgh bailie when he gave up the business around 1903, seemingly as a result of a downturn in the taxidermy trade. He and Jessie, who came from Balnaird, near Strathpeffer, had six children before she died aged 43, and he later remarried and became the father of two more. Those in the photo, submitted by Jessie's granddaughter Anne McArthur, of Dingwall, are thought by her to be Will, the eldest, Tom, the curly-haired boy and Jack. Mrs McArthur's mother, also Jessie, and two other sons, James and Hugh, arrived later, the latter becoming one of the Great War's many victims. Tom was very well known locally between the war years as an amateur actor, Rob Roy being among his starring roles at the old theatre in Bank Street and later at the Empire Theatre.

The Mellis family, who lived in Castle Street, shown in a studio photograph from the late 1890s. The picture can be dated to within a fairly short time frame, as the little boy in front, Charlie Mellis, born in 1890, was about eight. He died around 50 years ago, in his 70s, having been foreman fitter at the Inverness Lochgorm railway works, like his father before him. The parents' names are John and Charlotte. The tall young man is an older son Alexander. The girls in the picture are Polly, left, Charlotte and Helen, all of whom Linda remembers. The Mellis family home, together with some others on the west side of Castle Street, was destroyed in a landslide, when part of the Castle Hill subsided.

Another photo of members of the Mellis family Castle Street, pictured in the early 20th Century. In front are father John, son Alex and mother Charlotte, while behind are daughter-in-law Annie, her husband Charlie Mellis, and daughter Polly.

Members of the Mellis family, of Castle Street, pictured around the 1920s beside an old cannon outside Inverness Castle. On the far left, part of the wheel of a German howitzer, captured by the Cameron Highlanders at the Battle of Loos in 1915, is visible.

Inverness Girl Guides on parade between the wars. Fifth from the left is Eirwen Mellis, and the first name of the girl in front of her is Audrey.

Do you recognise yourself in this smartly turned-out squad? These are members of a class held for Inverness Boys' Brigade non-commissioned officers at BB headquarters, Washington Court, in 1957-58. In the picture, with a number after each, denoting which company to which he belonged, are, rear, from left: Lieutenant I MacDonald (1), C Nairne (6), H Coote (8), I Johnstone (3), G Bain (9), R Smith (3), R Colquhoun (1), A Ross (1), A Sutherland (7), R MacLean (5), G Ledingham (7), G MacDonald (6), D MacRae (6), A MacLennan (6), Captain E MacGillivray (5); front, from left: A MacBeath (9), P Home (4), J Crawford (9), J MacLellan (5) A MacGregor (1), S Lyall (1), Captain W J Godsman (6), J Nairne (9), Rev John Graham, St Marks, B Davidson (5), Lieutenant E MacKeddie (2), D Thomson (5), C MacKenzie (2), W MacDonald (5), G Cooper (2), J MacKenzie (7), R Mackay (2).

Members of Inverness Boys' Brigade Battalion pipe band practising at camp near Carrbridge in July 1955. The numbers in brackets indicate the companies to which each belonged. They are, left line, from front to rear: Finlay Mackenzie (5), Keith Birrell (5), George Stevenson (8), two unidentified boys part hidden; centre line: Bruce Balfour (5), Henry Nelson (6), Robert MacKay (2), Peter Home (4), Campbell Mackenzie (2); right line: Donald McGruer (7), Murray Thom (3), John Watson (5), Hugh Coote (8).

This photo of members of Inverness 3ʳᵈ Company Boys' Brigade, dates from about 1942 or 1943.

Youthful revellers at a third birthday party at Darris Road, Inverness, in 1977. The children, from left, are: Sara Jarvis, Ronald Grant, Lynn Jarvis, birthday boy Calum Morrison, Iain Morrison, Nicky Cruden, Mark Cruden.

Buildings in Peril

Within the past half century too much of byegone architecture which gave Inverness so much of its character has fallen to the demolishers' bulldozers.

Thankfully there are still many notable buildings in existence, but the architectural philistines are always ready to pounce, and the two featured on this page are quite literally in peril, the one having been severely damaged by fire three years ago, the other simply lying disused.

Both are now the subject of urgent restoration attempts by Highland Buildings Preservation Trust, a charitable, non profit-making organisation which acts as a "restorer of last resort" to save historic buildings at risk. Its aim is to secure a viable and appropriate end use for each building it restores, using any money raised from its sale to tackle other projects.

Born in Forres in 1803, Mitchell moved with his family in 1810 to Inverness, where he attended Inverness Royal Academy. He continued his studies in Aberdeen and in 1820 went to work on the construction of the Caledonian Canal, where his talents came to the attention of the engineering pioneer Thomas Telford, who appointed Mitchell his assistant.

When the railway age arrived in the Highlands, Mitchell conducted numerous line surveys and was involved in the construction of much of the early rail network north of Perth. He held the post of Inspector of Highland Roads and Bridges for 43 years from 1824, and also acted as engineer for the Scottish Fisheries Board. The author of several books, including Reminiscences of my Life in the Highlands, Mitchell retired in 1867, and died at his London home in November 1883. For much of last century Viewhill House was used as a youth hostel by the Scottish Youth Hostels Association. The ugly, intrusive front extension shows that Viewhill was already in the SYHA's possession when this photo, probably from the 1950s, was taken by the late Jimmy Nairn or one of his sons. In October 2007, after lying empty for some time, and on the verge of residential redevelopment, it was severely damaged by fire.

A survey conducted for Historic Scotland recently concluded that the shell of the building is capable of restoration.

Viewhill House, a B-listed mansion on Old Edinburgh Road, Inverness, dating from 1835, was for many years the home of Joseph Mitchell, the distinguished civil and railway engineer.

Merkinch Welfare Hall was built shortly before World War I by the Catch My Pal Union, an international interdenominational temperance movement, founded by Irish Presbyterian minister, the Rev Robert J Patterson, who waged a world-wide campaign against the demon drink.

It is a rare survival of a temperance meeting hall for young working men, who gathered there to play games in an alcohol-free environment. The movement enjoyed initial success in Inverness, with members organising concerts and public entertainment for good causes, but it has long since faded away.

The hall was also used in the hungry 1920s by redoubtable local midwife and nurse Isabella Davidson, whose story we told in Inverness Remembered V, to hold child-care classes for young mothers.

For some time in the later part of last century it was a venue for judo classes, but has lain unused for over 20 years, and is in poor condition. The Highland Buildings Preservation Trust has recently completed a feasibility study into the repair and re-use of the Welfare Hall and hopes that the building can be restored once again to the heart of the Merkinch community.

Football down the years

Of all games played in Inverness and district over the past century and a half, soccer has certainly been the most popular overall.

In recent years, due possibly to the availability of televised sport and the emergence of the couch potato, the game at its lower levels has arguably been to some extent in decline, with fewer shoestring-budget street and district teams, while shinty and rugby have shown some resurgence.

Perhaps however, the reason for football's endurance in the face of so many sophisticated diversions is that at its most basic, all that players require are a flat area of ground and a ball.

Whatever the factors involved, football has played a very important part in the life of Inverness, which currently boasts its own Premier League club, born from the marriage of two former Highland League sides, frequently opposing, and occasionally even beating such teams as the mighty Celtic and Rangers.

The year 1906 was certainly a successful one for Cluchnacuddin FC, whose team members are seen here proudly displaying the club's Highland League Champions' trophies. The only person we can identify immediately is the club president James Sinclair, sitting in the middle, whose grand-daughter Margaret Gordon, nee Sinclair, submitted this historic picture. Can any reader identify any of the players or committee members – and how many of these young men were still alive little over a decade later, after the Great War had taken its terrible toll on Inverness and the Highlands?

Pictured here with their trophy are the 1938-39 season members of Clachnacuddin FC, after they beat Babcock & Wilcox 5-3 in the final of the Scottish Qualifying Cup North, in November 1938. They are, rear, from left: F Lawson, Alick Wemyss, J Mapplebeck, J Baxter, W Bain, Billy Davidson; front, from left: George "Butch" Sinclair, Dullence Mackenzie, Roddie Maclean, Patsy Mackintosh, Nicol Munro. The club also topped the Highland League that season, the last full season before the war, with Buckie Thistle runners-up. How many of these young men were in uniform and far from their native burg on much more serious business only a short while later?

Clachnacuddin FC captain George "Butch" Sinclair receives the Scottish Qualifying Cup after his team beat Bab-cock & Wilcox 5-3 in November 1938.

Clach Rangers were understandably delighted to win the Inverness Rosebowl after beating Cameron Boys' Club 3-1 at the former Inverness Thistle ground. What was the year, and do any readers recognise any of the players? From the hairstyles, it seems to have been in the 1970s.

Clach Rangers' victorious under-16 team of 1955. Pictured here, with the Coronation Cup, are, rear, from left: George MacLeod, Terry McDonagh, Billy MacKenzie, Dougie Rodgers, Peter Home, Donnie MacLeod; front, from left: Donnie Grant, Alick MacLennan, Ernie Latham, John Stewart, Tommy Thomson.

Legendary Inverness Thistle FC chairman John S MacDonald (left), better known as Jock, and club vice-chairman George "Butch" Sinclair, pictured in May 1981 with the Inverness Cup, Qualifying Cup and Reserve Trophies.

Pictured here, at Inverness Station, is the award-winning LMS Scouts FC team of 1926. In the middle row, third from the left, is Andrew Shivas from Carlton Terrace, whose niece Pat Munro submitted this picture. Can any reader identify other members of the team?

St Joseph's School Primary 7 football team of 1974 – Rear row, from left: Billy Trace, Raymond Finlayson, Neil Morrison, James Trace, Malcolm MacLennan, Terence Van Reenan, Michael Black; front, from left: Neil -, ? Blackburn, unidentified, Bobo -, Wayne Van Reenan, Donnie Cameron, unidentified.

Inverness Caledonian FC Qualifying Cup Winners 1948-49. In this historic photo are, rear, from right: F Murchison (vice-president), E Fraser (outside-left), P MacKinnon (centre-half), J MacGillivray (right back); centre, from right: W Mackintosh (trainer), R Mackintosh (left-half), D Mackintosh (goalkeeper), D MacKenzie (centre-forward), D Robertson (right-half), - Munro (secretary); front, from right: - Galloway (left-back), J Fraser (inside-left), David Birrell (president) Bobby Bolt (captain and inside-right), F MacBeath (outside-right).

5th Boys' Brigade football team in the late 1940s. The lads pictured here are, rear, from left: D Macpherson, J Wardrope, F Mackenzie, S Macdonald, T Breadley; front, from left: M Smith, D MacDonald, T Wilson, G Imlah, R Clyne, D Forrest.

Craig Dunain Hospital football team from the building and engineering department who took part in a match against the male nurses. They are, rear, from left: S Fraser, M Urquhart, D Urquhart, D Grant, A Ross, J MacKenzie, M Smith; front, from left: J Mackay, J Nairn, R Lytham, J Mackenzie, G Bruce.

Inverness Boys' Brigade Battalion football team circa 1958: rear row, from left: Robert McAdam, Benjie MacDougall, James Dean, George Ross, Ian Philips, Tom Reilly; front, from left: Sandy MacBeath, John Summers, Billy Foley, Sandy Forbes, Denis Mackintosh.

A wee change from triumphant team photos is this crowd scene snapped at Caledonian FC's former ground in Telford Street, in the 1950s. Can any reader identify any of the spectators, does anyone know which team Caley was playing that day – and who won?

Quite literally in a league of their own were members of this scratch team recruited quickly by the Gellions Bar in 1957 to play some other group. Inverness exile Iain Cameron, now living in Winchester and a former regimental sergeant major in the Royal Army Pay Corps, who sent the photo in, says: "The match was a friendly, and who we played, or the final score, I cannot remember, but I do remember the great celebration we had in the Gellions afterwards." Team members were, rear, from left: Tommy Murdoch, - Murdoch, unidentified, mine host Niven Irvine, Donny Noble, Mike Jamieson and the team linesman, whose name Iain forgets; front, from left: Jack Curran, unidentified, Duncan Maclennan, Iain Cameron, Ernie Irvine.

Here's a mystery for local football buffs, together with some clues. The players in the photo are named from left, though with no distinction as to which row, as: Riggs, Stewart, Forsyth, Mackintosh, MacLeod, F R Munro, Purdon, Cameron, MacNeil (capt) Grant, Kinnaird. The cup in front is the Highland League Trophy, and the date, etched out on the cardboard backing, along with the players' names, is June 30, 1934. However, a check of the Highland League on Google shows that Buckie Thistle won the League in that year, while none of the names coincide with those of Buckie's star players of that era, nor does the strip, which seems closer to that of the "Lilywhites", Clach, although it is also similar to the away strip of the league runners-up that year, Forres Mechanics. So which team was it? And what was the year?

Other Sports

This photo of a team representing Inverness in a water polo tournament is thought to date from the early 1980s, but unfortunately we don't have the names of its members.

We're also short of names for this picture of end-of-season winners at Torvean Golf Club in th early 1980s.

The members of this foursome from Bishop's Road Bowling Club have obviously enjoyed a successful season, although the only one we can identify is Dan Macdonald, rear, right, whose granddaughter Eleanor Thomson, of Firthview Avenue, submitted the photograph, taken by local photographer D Whyte, whose studios chronicled the doings of local people for many decades in late Victorian days and last century. Nor do we know exactly the year it was taken, though it was probably shortly before World War II. Dan, who lived in Smith Avenue, and died in 1987, aged 79, was a very keen bowler.

Cricket was quite popular in Inverness of yesteryear during the summer months. These men are members of a local cricket club snapped in the inter-war years. The only member identified is Charlie Mellis, third from the left, sitting, whose granddaughter, Linda Law, lent us this photo.

Inverness Royal Academy athletics team of 1954, with sports trophies won during the session.

Jolly hockey-sticks with the girls of Inverness Royal Academy's hockey first eleven of 1955.

Inverness Royal Academy's sports day prizegiving in 1950, with in the centre, popular rector Donald J Macdonald (1900-93), from Lochcarron, who led the school ably between 1944 and 1962.

Schoolboy Graham Meeks prepares gingerly to dive into the deep end of the former swimming pool at Glebe Street during a swimming session around 1970, as others look on or dry themselves.

Many of the youngsters in this photo, taken at Lochardil Primary School sports in 1978, are now parents themselves and well advanced in their careers.

Merkinch Primary School hockey team 1966 – rear, from left: Eileen Wheeler, Eileen Donnachie, Sylvia Clark, Sandra Allan (A), Marie Mackenzie, Glynis Macrae. Front row, from left: Brenda Johnstone, Sandra Allan (B), Eleanor Ross, Mary Murchison, Margaret Wood, Pat Fraser.

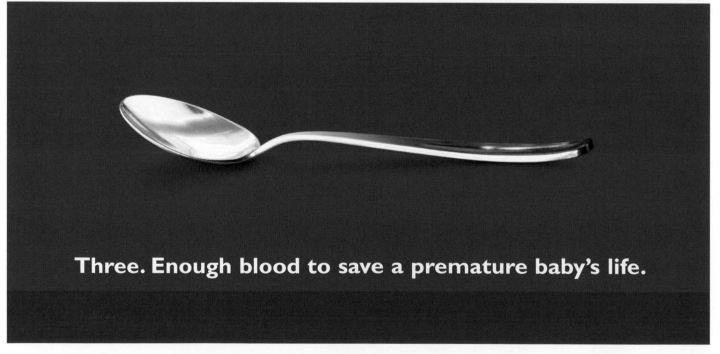

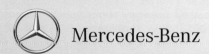

THE dores inn

Only a few miles from Inverness in Dores bay on the southern shores of Loch Ness is The Dores Inn, a traditional old coaching inn. With a recent refurbishment using old church chairs, leather sofas and a wood burning stove this great pub serves up amazing seasonal food sourced from local estates and producers. The Dores Inn Steak nights which happen on a Friday and Saturdays are well worth coming for – we are sourcing all our beef from a different region of Scotland each month giving you the opportunity to taste the flavours that regions create. In the bar we have real ales from many of Scotland's micro breweries and also a fine collection of malt whiskies. Outside a new patio has been created with a protective glass screen that has outstanding views across the loch – we look forward to welcoming you to the pub for breakfast, a coffee and cake, lunch or dinner or if you would like to stay in Dores there are superb B & B'S and self catering accommodation available and also the opportunity to drop anchor and row in.

Open 7 Days a week
10am till late
Tel. 01463 751203
www.thedoresinn.co.uk

Reminder
Call New Century Publishing regarding an idea for our new magazine
T. 01463 732225
E. s.barron@newcentury-pg.com

New Century
Publishing Group